How I Made 100 Times My Money in Real Estate in Seven Years

An Industry Veteran Takes You Alongside His Journey From $25,000 to $2,500,000, and Teaches You How to Be an Informed, Intelligent, Opportunity-Seizing Investor

Abe Oheb

Copyright 2019 Abe Oheb

All rights reserved. No part of this publication may be reproduced, distributed, or transmitted without the prior written permission of the publisher, except in the case of brief quotations embodied in critical reviews and certain other noncommercial uses permitted by copyright law.

Printed in the United States of America

First Edition

Limit of Liability/Disclaimer of Warranty: The publisher and the author make no representations or warranties with respect to the accuracy or completeness of the contents of this work and specifically disclaim all warranties, including without limitation warranties of fitness for a particular purpose. No warranty may be created or extended by sales or promotional materials. The advice and strategies contained herein may not be suitable for every situation. This work is sold with the understanding that the publisher is not engaged in rendering legal, accounting, or other professional services. If professional assistance is required, the services of a competent professional person should be sought. Neither the publisher nor the author shall be liable for damages arising herefrom.

Acknowledgments

Thank you Nilou for your help, and thank you Rodney for editing, designing, and printing this book.

Contents

Introduction 9
Part One: The Deals 11
    Deal #1 13
    Deal #2 20
    Deal #3 21
    Deal #4 26
    Deal #5 28
    My Equity in 2004 30
Part Two: Profitable Real Estate Investing - A Course 33
    Real Estate Investing - The Pluses and Minuses 35
        The Pluses 35
        The Minuses 38
    The Economic Cycle 40
    Increasing a Property's Value 41
    How to Research a Property 50
    Location 53

Zoning / Permitted Use 55
    Use and Change of Use 57
Finding Bargains 61
Foreclosures 63
Brokers and Negotiation Tactics 67
The P & S Agreement, Escrow, Contingency, and Due Diligence 70
Title 74
Financing 77
    Leverage 77
    Your Credit Score 79
    Types of Loans 81
    Getting a Loan 82
    Mortgage Payments 84
    Refinancing 85
Forms of Ownership 87
    Individual or Joint ownership 87
    Joint Venture 87
    Corporation 88
    LLC (Limited Liability Company) 89
Management 90
Tenants 93

- Types of Real Estate and Leases 96
  - Apartment buildings 97
  - Retail Properties..98
  - Office Buildings...100
  - Other 101
- CAP Rate and Return on Investment...................... 102
- Development... 105
- Attorneys and Legal Issues 107
- Income Taxes.. 109
- When to Sell..113
- Putting it All Together 116
- GLOSSARY 131

Introduction

I earned over 100 times my original investment through five real estate deals I made from 1997 to 2004. Looking back at my lengthy career in this industry, I feel like these five deals illustrate quite a bit about how to maximize profits through buying, enhancing, and selling properties. And I believe that anyone who invests in real estate can earn above average returns on their money, as long as they pay attention to opportunities, assess potential risks and rewards, use common sense, and look for ways to be quick and efficient.

Over the course of my career in real estate, I've made a habit of transforming lower end properties into highly profitable ones, often in a fairly brief period of time. And in this slim yet very informative book, I will share some of what I have learned during my many years in the business, including many tips and tricks that you will seldom find in real estate books or courses.

In Part One, I am going to detail the investments that yielded a 10,000% return over seven years. You'll get an up close look at how I made such staggering profits, and how you can too.

In Part Two, I will explain the essential ins and outs of the real estate game.

Part One: The Deals

Deal #1

In 1997, Los Angeles was in the process of recovering from an early 1990s recession marked by fires, a riot, a major earthquake, and a sluggish overall economy responsible for numerous real estate foreclosures and business bankruptcies.

It was then that a friend of mine told me about a building that was in foreclosure. For those of you not familiar with that term, a foreclosure is a process a lender uses in order to become the new owner of a property after the borrower fails to make payments on the property's loan.

The property was a four story mixed use building built in the 1920s, and was located in a populous, lower income neighborhood. The first floor was for retail use and had two tenants, while the upper floors consisted of 36 vacant and boarded up apartment units. The owner had completely neglected the building management for a long time, and ultimately abandoned the operation of the property altogether.

I did some research at City Hall, where I learned that the upper residential floors were cited by the Los Angeles city "task force" due to numerous health, fire, and building violations. The owner of the building had failed to comply with city orders, and the tenants responded by taking legal action against the owner. The owner decided that his best option was to close up the apartment units, abandon the property, and allow the lender to begin the foreclosure proceedings.

Keep in mind that although most real estate owners try to avoid foreclosure, there are times when a foreclosure might be preferable to holding on to a property. In the case of this property, the owner's original loan was for $900,000, back in 1989 when the property had a value of $1.5 million. However, by 1997, the property was worth about $350,000, while the loan amount had increased to $1.1 million due to back interest and penalties. In other words, the owner owed $1.1 million on a $350,000 property, and his net equity in the investment was negative $750,000. Furthermore, at the time, the property wasn't taking in enough money to cover its expenses and its loan payments. And finally, since the building was deemed non-compliant by the city of Los Angeles, whoever owned it faced potential fines and lawsuits in the future. So all in all, the owner was very motivated to let the lender take over the property.

During my investigation with the city of Los Angeles, I also found out that the owners had missed five years of property tax payments, and several years of Department of Water & Power (DWP) payments. (Like many older apartment buildings, this building had common electrical and water meters, making the owner responsible for paying for the tenants' electricity and water usage.) Due to non-payment of property taxes and DWP charges, the county of Los Angeles treasurer scheduled the property to be auctioned in February 1998, in order for the county and city to recover money owed to them.

My plan was to contact the lender before the foreclosure took place, so I could purchase the loan against the property. In other words, I wanted to buy the loan, and then foreclose on the property and take over the ownership. However, after doing a lot of research, I found out that the original lender on record did not even exist anymore. Keep in mind that in the early to mid 90s, many financial institutions had gone bankrupt due to the poor economy. They would go out of business, and another bank or institution would purchase their assets.

In the case of this property, the loan/note had changed hands four times, and most likely sold as part of a bundle containing a mixture of many good loans and some bad ones. The previous three owners had not foreclosed on the property, since they were aware of its non-compliant status, and they didn't want to assume any future liabilities. All three financial institutions chose to simply retain the loan/note, despite its non-performing status. The current owner was a large bank in Palm Beach, Florida. And as you might imagine, they were highly motivated to pretty much just get rid of the loan/note.

I reported the building's various physical, financial, and legal problems to the bank in Florida, and after two weeks of discussions and negotiations, they sold the note to me for only $25,000.

I decided to bring partners into the deal, since I prefer and enjoy working with other people. At the time, not that many people were interested in investing in unstable California real estate—but I did eventually manage to find a couple of partners.

We paid $25,000 for a $1.1 million note. It seems like a phenomenal deal—but keep in mind that it was possible the county would foreclose on the property before we did, because as I mentioned earlier, the property owed quite a bit in unpaid property taxes and DWP charges.

Even though my partners and I were just the note holders and we didn't have official control of the building's operations, I decided to take over the property anyways. I devoted my efforts to the first floor retail units, which were currently occupied by tenants with month-to-month leases—and in very little time, I was able to raise the total rental income from $3,000 to $5,000 a month, while incurring virtually no operating expenses. As for the 36 upper floor apartment units, I just kept them boarded up, since they were in such a deteriorated state. (They had been ransacked so many times, that even their copper sprinkler pipes had been torn out of the walls and sold as scrap metal.)

Shortly after purchasing the note, I also attempted to contact the borrower/owner, who was also the guarantor of the note, and owed us $1.1 million on paper. I couldn't find him—but I did track down his daughter, who informed us that the owner had no intention of giving us any money.

Our options were to either (a) file a judicial foreclosure on the borrower/owner and demand payment of the $1.1

million, or (b) file a regular foreclosure in order to simply gain ownership of the property. We figured the first option would require lots of time and money, and might not lead to us getting anything other than the property. That being the case, we ended up going with the quicker and less expensive route of a regular foreclosure.

Instead of owning the building under our own names, we created a Limited Liability Company (LLC). An LLC is more or less an independent company that isn't tied to your personal assets. I also consulted with county and city officials, who told me that as long as I kept the apartment units boarded up, I would not expose myself to any liabilities.

Our LLC owned the building outright, and was pulling in a decent sized income through rent from the two retail units. However, the building owed $200,000 in unpaid property taxes, and $100,000 in unpaid DWP (Department of Water & Power) fees. In California and most other states, if you don't pay property taxes, the county will put a lien on the property, and auction it to the public after five years of non payment. If the highest bid is less than the taxes owed, the city will pull the property from auction, and then auction it again the following year. If a sale is made, the government gets its money owed, and then any money left over goes to the lender and owner.

If the auction had gone through, my partners and I would've bid on the property, knowing that it was taking in a substantial amount of income, and it had potential to make even more in the future. However, the state did not proceed with the auction (—possibly because there was a change in California law regarding DWP liens on properties).

My next move was to file an appeal with the county in order to reduce our property taxes due. I stated that the property had been taxed according to its old value, even though its actual value had plummeted over time. The county assessor agreed, and adjusted the rate charged for the past five years, cutting $40,000 of the $200,000 due.

I continued increasing the building's rents as the local economy improved, and in 1998, my partners and I sold the property for $440,000. After paying off all the money the building owed such as property taxes, we were left with about $230,000.

Deal #2

We avoided paying income taxes on our profit from Deal #1 by using what's known as a "1031 exchange," and we purchased another property using the proceeds from the previous sale.

I located a boarded up four story building that used to be operated as a swap meet. We bought it for $275,000—a bit more than the money we got from the last property—and we immediately made a variety of important repairs and enhancements. We then sectionalized the first floor into fourteen booths and rented them out as swap meet units, yielding us $10,000 a month in rental revenues. In the meantime, we applied for a permit to use one of the booths as a restaurant, particularly because a restaurant would greatly boost the number of people drawn to the swap meet. Later, we also began opening more booths on the building's upper floors.

As we continued to increase the property's rental revenue, a prospective buyer expressed interest in the building, and in 1999 we sold it for $520,000 cash.

Deal #3

With the proceeds in hand from our last sale, my partners and I made another 1031 exchange, and purchased another similar property in the same area: an old brick structured mixed use building with 36 apartment units and three first floor retail units. We bought it for just $830,000—but keep in mind that (a) the units were subject to rent control laws (in other words, there was a local law that said rents on existing tenants could not be raised more than a certain amount per year), and (b) the building was somewhat deteriorated. The owner probably felt like there was no point in fixing up the place, since he couldn't legally raise rents on the tenants there. He ended up neglecting the building so much, that it did not have a working heating system, which is a violation of building owners' maintenance requirement laws. This gave me great negotiating leverage with the seller. Not only did we buy the building for a low price, the seller gave us a five year $435,000 loan with an 8% interest rate. (I should also point out that the seller himself had gotten a low interest $167,000 loan on the building in 1986 from the City of

Los Angeles Redevelopment Agency—so he was lending us that money at a markup.)

I took over the building with an objective of maximizing my profits while operating within the confines of rent control laws. Before I get into that, let me talk about rent control laws in general.

Many regions in the US have certain laws that place limits on the rate a building owner can increase tenant rents. In Los Angeles, all apartment buildings built prior to 1978 are under rent control, and this restricts landlords from increasing a current tenant's rent more than an annual rate set by the city—usually around 4%. In other words, if the rent during year 1 of the lease is $500, then the rent during year 2 cannot be raised to more than $520 ($500 + 4%).

However, whenever a tenant moves out, the owner can charge the new tenant any rent. And then from that point on, the rent will be subject to rent control again. So, if a tenant is paying $500 a month and then he moves out, the owner can legally rent the same unit to another person for whatever the market allows—let's say $1,000 a month. But the following year, he can only raise that new tenant's rent to $1,040 ($1,000 plus 4%). The unit is once again subject to rent control until the second tenant moves out and is replaced with another tenant.

Now, let's say that over several years, the economy weakens and then becomes strong again. At first, the rent for a unit is $1,000. A few years later, the owner has lowered the rent significantly, due to the weakened economy. No one will rent the unit for more than $500—so he signs a one year lease with someone for $500 a month. Four years later, the economy is strong again. There are people out there willing to pay $1,000 a month for the unit. However, the unit has been occupied by the same tenant for the last four years—and due to rent control laws, his rent has only been raised 4% per year. In other words, he's paying $585 for a $1,000 unit. Or let's consider another scenario where the state of the economy didn't necessarily change that much. The tenant started off paying $1,000 a month for a unit, and his rent was raised at a rate of 4% per year. Meanwhile, local real estate prices increased at a rate of 6% per year. Ten years into that, his rent is $1480 a month—but the unit is worth $1790 a month.

As you can see, rent control laws can cause rents to be and stay artificially low—as in, lower than what they would be due to open market supply and demand. When you purchase a building that's subject to rent control, some of the tenants will be legally entitled to artificially low rents.

In my own case, Building #3 had plenty of units in that category. On the other hand, it also had several units that were vacant, and we were also aware that several other tenants would be moving out in the near future. So although we were still constrained by rent control laws, it was evident that all in all, we had plenty of opportunities to achieve high rents and it was to our advantage to enhance the building,

Upon purchasing the property, my partner and I quickly made a variety of improvements. One, of course, was the legally required repair of the building heating system, which dated back to the 1920s, and used a steam heater, plus radiators in the units which were removed from the rooms decades ago and stored in the basement. We reattached all the radiators and made the original steam heater operable and provided heat to the tenants.

We also repainted the building's exterior, repaired common areas like the lobby and hallways, and built a new laundry room from scratch.

Not long after taking over the building, we increased the total monthly rental revenue by 30%, and sold the property in 2002 for $1,175,000. The buyer paid us $350,000 down, and we loaned him the remaining $825,000 for 5 years with an 8% fixed interest rate.

(Keep in mind that we ourselves still had a loan with the previous owner that was for five years and $435,000, at an 8% interest rate. So after selling our property, we would be receiving payments on the money we lent to the new owner, and we'd also be making payments on the money we borrowed from the previous owner.)

Deal #4

A couple of weeks after selling building #3, we purchased a 37-unit apartment building for $1,000,000, paying $300,000 down, and taking out a purchase loan for $700,000 from a bank. Since we had gotten a $350,000 down payment after selling the last property, and we made a $300,000 down payment on this new property, we had $50,000 left over, which we planned to use for building improvements.

We made several major changes to the building shortly after purchasing the building. I'll describe one of them in detail, since it's unique and it really illustrates how an owner should explore opportunities to enhance his properties.

When we purchased the building, the basement was out of use and only accessible from a stairway inside the building. In order to make the basement an income producing space, we constructed a new way to access it from the property's front on a busy street. And since the building was located in a commercial zone, we were able to rent the space to someone who wanted to start a high end art studio and was willing to pay a fairly high rent per square foot.

This one change was singlehandedly responsible for a dramatic increase in the building's overall value.

While we were converting the basement, the owner of Building #3 paid off the entire balance of the $825,000 loan he had with us, even though that money was not due for a long time. He most likely was able to obtain another loan with better terms, so he used the proceeds from that loan to pay off the one he had with us.

This unexpected move by him required us to pay some capital gains taxes that year, even though we had originally intended to defer those taxes. After paying the taxes, were left with $425,000 cash to invest.

Deal #5

While still owning Building #4, we purchased a single family home. I normally don't deal in such properties—but with this one, I saw the potential to make a quick profit by flipping it. The home was in a good neighborhood in West Los Angeles, it had a high quality layout, and it hadn't been renovated since being built in the 1960s. The market for homes in the area was also red hot—so I knew we'd have no problem selling a new looking house in that area for a fairly high price.

We acquired the house in November of 2003 for $1,100,000, and immediately began the transformation. We spent about $100,000 repairing walls, ceilings, and floors, painting the exterior and interior, building a new roof, working on the landscaping, and completely changing the bathrooms and kitchen.

The purchase and renovation of the home was financed by the loan payoff mentioned in the last chapter, as well as the operating income from Property #4.

Five months later in March of 2004, the renovation was complete. We put it in the market for $1,800,00, went into escrow for $1,640,000 after 3 months, and closed the deal in July of 2005.

After paying commissions and loan fees as well as the $700,00 loan, we netted $643,000, and transferred that into an accommodator account for exchange. (If you intend to make a 1031 exchange, you must deposit all the proceeds of the sale with an accommodator until you find a new property.)

My Equity in 2004

In 2004, we still owned building #4. Its income was increased by 40% and its market value was $2,500,000—and, after subtracting our current $700,000 loan in the property, it left us $1,800,000 in equity.

At that time in 2004 we also had $643,000 with the accommodator for exchange, plus an additional $50,000 in accumulated operating income from building #4.

So in summary, in 1997 we originally invested $25,000 in a non-performing real estate loan, and within seven years, we had converted it into $2,500,000 of cash and real estate equity.

This happened through a proactive approach, as opposed to a passive one. My philosophy regarding real estate is as follows. As a real estate investor, your job is not to merely buy property and wait for the market to increase the value of your property. Rather, it's imperative that you consider all available opportunities for maximizing your profits. Utilize whatever can help you gain an edge. When looking for properties to buy, be very mindful of whether a building has the potential to earn above average returns via improvements, rental increases, etc. Consider the various ways you can come to acquire the property and finance the deal. Explore options available when it comes to dealing with creditors and local laws and codes.

Real estate investing is not at all like stock market investing. Granted, both investments have you owning something that tends to increase in value significantly over the long run. That's a primary selling point when it comes to both stocks and real estate. That being said, stock market investing involves merely owning a business, whereas real estate investing involves owning and operating a business. And as I've illustrated in this section's five examples, it's in the operation that you can take various measures to turn ordinary profits into extraordinary profits.

Part Two: Profitable Real Estate Investing - A Course

Real Estate Investing - The Pluses and Minuses

The Pluses

Very few industries have as much money making potential as real estate. The typical property earns a 6% annual return through rental revenues. The property itself also increases in value at a rate of about 5% a year on its own. Furthermore, investors can borrow money and increase their returns even more. If you buy a building with your own money, you yield the 6% income along with the 5% building appreciation. But suppose you borrow money from the bank in order to buy the property, and you pay an interest rate of 5% on that money. You pay 5% on the money you borrow, but you make more than 5% on that money. In other words, you earn a return on money that isn't even yours. And of course, as mentioned earlier, if you buy a property that shows the potential for improvement, you can enhance the property, decrease vacancies, and raise rents—and that can make the building appreciate considerably more than 5% a year.

So, suppose you buy a $1 million property with $200,000 of your own money and $800,000 borrowed from a bank. You also spend $100,000 in order to improve the property's condition, and you take advantage of every opportunity to raise rents. Your investment is $300,000 ($200,000 on a down payment and $100,000 in building improvements). And over the first three years, you collect $500,000 in rent, and you spend $250,000 on loan payments and other expenses. Your net cash flow is $250,000. And again—this is on an initial investment of $200,000 down and $100,000 in building improvements. Furthermore, the building's value has increased to $1.4 million, due to the enhancements you've made, the increase in rental revenue, and the fact that real estate in the area has appreciated at a rate of 5% per year. You spent $1.1 million on the property (the $1 million purchase price plus the $100,000 in enhancements), and the current value is $1.4 million—which amounts to a $300,000 increase in equity.

So in summary, on an initial investment of $300,000, you took in a net of $250,000 cash via the rental income, plus, your property's value appreciated by $300,000.

And also keep in mind that you did it without many of the demands that come with other types of businesses. Now, I'm not saying real estate is always a walk in the park. But suppose instead of buying a property, you use your $300,000 to open a store or restaurant. Operating that kind of business usually involves a demanding schedule, whereas with a real estate investment, there are many occasions where you can work when you want.

It's also possible to succeed in this industry without a wide general skill set. With other types of businesses, you as the owner/operator might have a very tough time getting ahead if you don't possess numerous general skills—for instance, interpersonal, mathematical, organizational, persuasional, memory, and communicational skills. In real estate, there are many examples of people performing at a high level and making millions of dollars despite not having high skill levels in these general areas.

The Minuses

Okay. I've painted real estate in a very positive light. Now let's look at the less desirable aspects of real estate investing. One is that your investment is not so liquid. You can't quickly convert your real estate investment into cash, the way you can with stocks, bonds, T-bills, CDs, etc. Also, every real estate transaction is accompanied by significant fees (broker fees, bank fees, etc.) And the transactions take time—unlike, say, a stock trade. Also keep in mind that real estate investments don't offer guarantees or anything close to them. Revenues and property values fluctuate—and if you borrow money, those fluctuations can be huge.

If you want extremely steady, reliable income, then real estate might not be for you.

Real estate investing also involves making many decisions that involve numerous factors, it requires you to have a hands on approach when it comes to finding, making, and managing an investment, and it also requires you to deal with a variety of people, such as buyers, sellers, bankers, attorneys, brokers, contractors, engineers, managers, tenants, architects, and city officials. That being said, you can hire or partner up with others who can handle many of these people and tasks.

So, as a real estate investor, you need to either (a) make decisions, actively manage a venture, and deal with a variety of people, or (b) have the willingness and ability to find others who can do this for you.

The Economic Cycle

The US government and the Federal Reserve Bank use various measures to minimize economic fluctuations and make the economy grow at a steady rate. But despite these efforts, the economy tends to move along unpredictably, and there's really no reliable way to tell when the economy is going to encounter a recession or when it's going to grow quickly. Instead of trying to predict what the economy will do, it's better to just focus on doing your job as a real estate investor. Buy properties that show the potential to earn above average returns. Take advantage of all opportunities to enhance the value of your property. When the economy is weak, you'll find more in the way of certain kinds of bargains. When the economy is strong, you'll come across better opportunities to quickly enhance and flip properties. Furthermore, if your property values increase on account of a strong economy, you can refinance your existing loan and get the benefit of tax-free cash (which I'll explain later).

Increasing a Property's Value

The value of a property increases and decreases due to these factors:

- inflation or deflation

- the state of the local economy

- The state of the national and world economy

- alterations made to the neighborhood

- the perceived desirability of the neighborhood (in other words, is the region hot or cold, trendy or not trendy?)

- any changes made to the property (enhancements or deterioration)

- any changes in revenue and expenses

Many of these factors are beyond a property owner's control. That being said, an owner has opportunities to enhance his building, and also to increase the building's profits (through enhancement or through other means). Instead of settling for a return that matches the average in the area, he can focus on making property improvements and increasing the rental income.

Before I get into more advanced ways to achieve higher income for your property, I'll start by talking about something very basic: raising rent on an existing tenant. As an owner, you need to know what the contract allows, what local laws allow, and the going rates for comparable units in similar buildings. You also need to consider whether the tenant is a quality tenant—as in, someone who behaves well and pays his rent on time. In most cases, retaining good tenants is a fundamental component of successful real estate investing and management—and your approach to lease negotiation should reflect that.

If a tenant's lease is up, his rent under the old contract is $800 a month, and his unit is now worth $1,000 a month, you should by all means increase his rent as soon as possible.

That being said, if you are dealing with a high quality tenant, you might want to only raise his rent to $950, and perhaps also do something for the tenant in return for the rent increase—for instance, repaint his unit, or make a minor repair that isn't necessary. Make an effort to retain a high quality tenant. After all—if the tenant moves out, not only will you incur expenses in order to fill the unit, the new tenant might not be as good as your current one. You should be willing to occasionally rent at below market rates for the sake of having better tenants and a low turnover rate.

Now, suppose you have an existing tenant who is somewhat undesirable, and his lease is up. In such a case, instead of increasing his rent from $800 to $950 (like you did with the high quality tenant), you might be better off increasing it to $1,050, even though the unit is only worth $1,000 on the open market. In other words, you create a situation that either (a) has the less desirable tenant pay an inflated rent, or (b) has that tenant move out so you can rent his unit for $1,000 to a more desirable tenant (;—as opposed to (c) renting the unit for $1,000 to the less desirable tenant).

The point is, your terms and conditions should be adjusted to account for the quality level of the tenant.

And getting back to the original point, it's important to raise rents as soon as possible, and to know the open market value of a unit when negotiating the new rental rate.

But of course, if you want to earn above average returns on a consistent basis, it's not enough to merely wait for leases to expire and then attempt to raise rents when market conditions, laws, and contracts allow it.

There are many other ways to add value to a property. Savvy investors can recognize certain types of potential that go unnoticed by most people, and they also find ways to make changes in a quick and efficient manner. This often requires creativity, imagination, and seeing things from a new, not-so-common perspective.

You might, for instance, see an industrial building for sale, and realize that it can be transformed into an apartment, retail, or office building that commands much higher rents per square foot. Or you might buy a 2,000 square foot home knowing you can add a bedroom to it for $20,000, and thereby increase the property's value by $50,000.

Here's a more typical example involving a multi-family property. Suppose you come across an older rent-controlled apartment building with two vacancies. Due to the rent control laws, most of the tenants are renting units for well below market value—say, for about $500, when those units would command $1,000 on the open market. Since the rents are low and rent control laws are in place, the open market value of the building is not particularly high on a per unit basis. It can be purchased for way less than similar buildings with no rent control laws, or rent controlled buildings in which the rents are considerably higher. You buy the building with the intention of increasing the rental revenue 30-50% within the next couple of years. You start by renovating the two vacancies and renting them for $1,000 a month. You also adopt a strategy of getting many of the $500 a month tenants to move out. This involves two approaches. First, you try to evict tenants who have breached their rental contract due to non payments or late payments of rent, excessive noise, overcrowding, etc. As for the tenants who cannot be evicted, you offer them a substantial sum of money to move out. (Keep in mind that there might be local laws regulating these types of payments.) And as soon as anyone is evicted or moves out, you renovate their unit and rent it for $1,000 a month.

The amount of value you create in this way is considerably more substantial than it might appear at first glance.

Suppose your building has 20 units total, and over the course of two years, you have eight rent-controlled tenants move out, and you replace them with eight new tenants paying open market rates. The average rent for those eight units increases from $500 to $1,000. That amounts to an additional $48,000 per year in rental revenue ($500 increase x 8 units x 12 months). If your property is taking in an additional $48,000 per year, in a certain sense that means the value of your property has increased by about $480,000 (assuming it's in a typical US residential neighborhood). Now let's consider the expenses associated with changing those eight tenants and increasing rents. Evicting a tenant or paying him to move out, renovating a unit, not receiving rent for a few months, finding a new tenant, etc.—that amounts to about $15,000 per unit, or $120,000 for all eight units in your property. That means by spending $120,000, you have increased the value of your property by $480,000 via eight rent increases. That's a profit of $360,000—and this is on an initial investment (down payment) of, say, $600,000. Also, the expenses you incur (on evictions, renovations, etc.) are paid for with the cash flow from the other units.

(Keep in mind that before buying any property, you must first check with local city authorities to find out if certain improvements and changes are allowable and meet all city codes. These laws differ greatly from property to property, and they will often determine whether a property is a good investment, or one that can expect to earn an average return.)

As a real estate investor, one thing to keep in mind is that if you want to maximize your return on investment, it's important to spend money properly.

Right now, let's consider expenditures that fall under the general category of property improvement. Within that general category, there are numerous specifics, such as

- New facades and/or storefronts

- Interior or exterior painting

- Insulation

- New roofing

- New elevators

- Replacement of kitchen cabinets, appliances, bathroom fixtures, etc.

- New pipes

- Electrical work

- Additions to the property

- An extensive renovation or remodeling of the property

An owner must know how and where to spend his/her allocated property improvement funds in order to maximize his property's income and market value.

In many cases, this should be dictated by the preferences of tenants—and that includes current tenants, as well as any future tenants you anticipate having or trying to attract. Existing tenants care more about plumbing, air conditioning, and major kitchen appliances than they do about whether the building's cosmetic appearance is up to par.

If you know how to spend money properly, this can give you a huge edge in increasing your overall return on investment. Keep in mind that this sometimes involves spending money on non-standard building enhancements.

In Deal #4 in part 1 of this book, we bought a 36 unit apartment building on Sunset Boulevard with a large basement with no use. Since the property is zoned commercial, I brought the dead space to life by fixing it up and by building a stairway providing direct access from Sunset Boulevard. It took six months to do this, and cost $8,000. I leased the new space to an art studio business for $1475 a month, or $17,700 a year—and that increased rental income boosted the property's market value by over $200,000.

How to Research a Property

Here's what I recommend doing whenever you come across a property that you might want to purchase.

- Familiarize yourself with the property's neighborhood. Get a sense of what the local market is like. Drive around the area (preferably with an experienced broker) during the day and also at night, and examine nearby properties that are for sale or rent.

- Examine the physical state of the building and its environment. Walk into all vacant units.

- Consider what kinds of enhancements you can make to the property, the various ways you can increase revenue or decrease expenses, and what it will take to change the building and its profits in those ways.

- Go through the property's profit and loss statements.

- Calculate the property's value, using recent sales of comparable buildings as a starting guideline.

- Consider the following:

  - How much money do you have available to invest?

  - Can you bring partners into the venture?

  - How much money do you need for any required remodeling?

  - Do you have the time and experience to remodel the building?

  - Who is going to manage the operations of the building?

  - Are you interested in and familiar with the property type?

  - How will you obtain financing?

- Determine the potential risk and reward associated with making your investment and carrying through your plan.

- Consider whether you can deal with an economic downturn. In other words, if the rental revenue decreases by, say, 30%, and the property becomes cash flow negative, will you be able to infuse money into the property in order to meet its financial obligations?

Location

Although the location of a property has a great deal of significance to a real estate investor, your motto shouldn't be "location, location, location," but rather, "profit, profit, profit."

Location is one of several factors that must be gauged in order to determine a property's current and future value, and potential for creating value.

In the scope of this, some characteristics of a good location include:

(a) A deteriorated property surrounded by buildings that are in good condition. This indicates that significant value can be quickly added by bringing the building up to the standard of neighboring properties.

(b) A lower end neighborhood that is being improved by the private sector or the government, to the point where lower income residents are being replaced with higher income residents

(c) An area undergoing job growth or and other economic growth

(d) A property that has satisfactory access to the building

(e) Advantageous laws regarding zoning and the permitted / allowed use of properties

Zoning / Permitted Use

Almost all cities in the US designate segments of their city into zones. Each zone has its own rules regarding what types of real estate development and modifications are permissible. For instance, within a city, only some zones allow the construction of a high rise office building. After all—the city wouldn't want a developer to build a property like that right next to someone's house.

Cities have zoning maps of the real estate within the city, and they also have a building code book. Zoning and building codes regulate what can be built on a given lot—as in, the building type and density.

For instance, in the city of Los Angeles, an "R4" zoning designation indicates that you may build 100 multifamily units per acre, whereas R3 signifies that you may build 50 units per acre. (Real estate laws vary from city to city. What an R4 zoning allows you to build on a lot in one city may be different in another city with the same designation.) There are also codes listed that describe requirements regarding maximum and/or minimum height, setback, and parking spaces.

Keep in mind that even in the case of four properties located at the same intersection, each one might be subject to much different rules.

Also consider how zoning and codes are subject to changes, and these changes can greatly increase or decrease a property's value. Decreases are more common, since the majority of zoning and code changes involve the addition of restrictions. That being said, these changes tend to be slow moving, and there is plenty of advance warning of a coming change. Furthermore, if you own a property that was built according to previous zoning and building codes, and they change, your building might be "grandfathered"—in other words, you can maintain the building as is, without bringing it up to the new code. However, safety codes such as fire and health codes are not grandfathered. In these situations, the city gives the owner ample time to bring his property up to the new fire and safety codes.

One more thing to keep in mind is that in the case of all zoning laws, a property owner may make a request for zoning modifications or relief from a zoning ordinance under what's known as a "zoning variance."

Real estate investors need to be attentive to zoning ordinances and code restrictions regarding the use of properties. In assessing a property, it's important to find out what local laws will allow you to do when it comes to changing the use of a property, and adding units and/or square footage.

Be aware that it is not enough to check a property's zoning designation. You also need to contact the city (usually the Department of Building and Safety) in order to get a complete and accurate sense of what is and isn't allowed. What they tell you might differ significantly from what the zoning designation states.

Use and Change of Use

Allowed Use is one of the most important characteristics of a property. Whether you are buying vacant land for development, or a property that you intend to alter, the use and ultimately change of use of an existing building affects its value a great deal.

In the case of vacant land you should know what you're allowed to build. In the case of the existing structure, you should know what you're allowed to add to the building, as well as what other uses are allowed aside from the current one.

The local marketplace for real estate changes over time, and this often involves a major change in the demand for or supply of a particular category, such as office spaces, condominiums, or retail spaces. In some cases, having the option to change the use of a property can have a substantial amount of value—because, for instance, it might be highly advantageous to convert an office building into condominiums or apartments/lofts, or a Victorian home into a medical office, or a storage space into a showroom, or the first floor of an office building into retail spaces.

(Before embarking on such a course, you should check with the city and find out whether the local zoning allow the change of use, and whether you have enough parking spaces for the new use.)

Sometimes you purchase a property with the specific intention of changing its use. A few years ago in various areas of Los Angeles, it was profitable to purchase vacant warehouses or factory buildings and convert them into swap meets. Let's consider a typical example. There is a vacant warehouse listed for $700,000. If the warehouse is rented to a tenant, it will generate $70,000 in annual revenues and incur $15,000 in expenses, leaving a profit of $55,000. An investor purchases the vacant warehouse for $700,000, with the intention of converting it to a swap meet. He spends $200,000 on the conversion, making his total investment $900,000. And upon converting the property, he rents the spaces for $150,000 a year, and he incurs $25,000 a year in operating expenses. His annual income amounts to $125,000, on a $900,000 initial investment. Contrast this to making $55,000 on a warehouse with an initial investment of $700,000.

As you can see, a change of use can boost an investor's rate of return considerably. In the example mentioned, the conversion incurred expenses of $200,000, and increased annual profits by $70,000. The investor was able to see the potential for increased profits by considering supply and demand as it applied to a certain neighborhood. In this case, he determined that the area's demand for swap meets (and retail spaces in general) was high and the supply was low. Meanwhile, the converse was true for warehouses: there was an ample supply of them in the area, but the demand was relatively low. That led him to the conclusion that it could be advantageous to convert a warehouse into a swap meet. And after plugging in some numbers that could forecast the annual rental revenue and expenses of a swap meet, he figured that he could earn a high return on his money by purchasing the warehouse for $700,000 and converting it for $200,000.

Finding Bargains

Aside from finding ways to increase the value of a property, it's also generally a good idea to try and buy real estate for below its current market value. I say generally, because sometimes paying full price for a hot or high potential property is just fine. But there are also plenty of cases where bargain hunting can be the ideal option.

One way to find bargains is to seek out sellers who really need the money for whatever reason. Some owners are highly motivated to sell their property soon, while others have a completely different attitude, and think something like, "If it sells at a good price, fine. But if I don't get any takers, that's OK, too; I'll just hang on to the property for the time being." If a seller is in the middle of a divorce, he's moving, he wants to raise funds for another investment, or he's having cash flow problems in general, he might be willing to sell a property for less than it's worth.

If you want to identify owners that fall in the category of "highly motivated," you can't rely on brokers. Brokers seldom give you a clear, accurate sense of why the owner is selling his property. It's better to meet the property owner and perform your own firsthand investigation.

Foreclosures

(Every state has different laws and procedures, regarding foreclosures—but in this book, I'll focus on the general process without getting into any specific legal details.)

When an owner fails to make payments on his loan for more than three straight months, the lender will send him a warning of default, which will be followed by a notice of default, which will in turn be followed by the lender making a current appraisal of the property (in other words, the lender will try to determine how much the property is worth on the open market), and then send a notice of foreclosure, and a legal request for payment of the mortgagee's balance due. If payment is not made, the court will assign a receiver to the property, who will collect rents, pay urgent expenses, and give the remainder of the money to the lender. The court will eventually auction the property to the public.

Now, suppose the balance due on the mortgage is $800,000 (including penalties, accumulated interest, etc.), and the property sells for $1,000,000 at auction. In such a case, $800,000 will go to the lender, and $200,000 will go to the owner. But suppose the highest bid at the auction is $700,000—which is $100,000 less than the mortgage balance due. In this case, the property will not be sold to the highest bidder. Instead, the ownership of the property will be legally transferred from the current owner to the lender. As for the $100,000 difference between property value (the highest bid, $700,000) and the mortgage's balance due ($800,000), that is what's known as a "shortfall deficiency." If the borrower has personally guaranteed the loan, he will owe that $100,000 to the lender.

Keep in mind that during the foreclosure process, the owner always has the right to pay his mortgage balance due, and stop the property from being foreclosed. He might also find some legal means of postponing the auction. Another option is for the owner to try and negotiate some sort of settlement with the lender. This option is especially common when the economy is weak and banks are not looking to take over a property. A fourth option is for the property owner to declare bankruptcy, in which case the law will give him additional time to "reorganize." A fifth option is for the owner and lender to form a settlement that involves ownership going from the owner to the lender, without an actual legal foreclosure. In other words, the bank might tell an owner, "Your property is worth $700,000, and you owe us $800,000—but if you give us the property and $50,000 cash, we won't foreclose, and your credit won't be affected." This is what's known as an "in lieu foreclosure."

As a building owner, if you find yourself unable to make payments on your loan, going through a foreclosure or one of the options above will require a considerable amount of time and effort—and you might lose your initial investment in the property, and end up with a much lower credit score. Seek the advice of a competent attorney who has enough experience in foreclosures to handle your case. Obviously, your aim is to avoid a loan default altogether—but in real estate, some investments don't work out. In such a case, explore all your options, and see which one suits you best.

As a real estate buyer, an owner's loan defaults can lead to you getting a good deal—but keep in mind that such good deals aren't necessarily that easy to find. Just because a building is being foreclosed, that doesn't automatically mean some buyer out there is going to get a good deal. Also keep in mind that in dealing with such properties, you often have to pay all cash to take over them, and they might be in poor condition and/or have many vacancies.

Brokers and Negotiation Tactics

There are two ways to buy or sell real estate.

The **direct** method does not involve brokers. Many owners will simply put "For Sale By Owner" signs on their property, and/or in some sort of online or newspaper listing.

The **broker** method involves a seller signing an exclusive agreement with a broker who will list the property and take a commission (usually 5-6%) should it sell. The broker in this case is called the listing broker or seller's broker. When dealing with a broker, a buyer can either use the seller's broker, or he can bring in his own buyer's broker, in which case the commission will be split between the two brokers. In either case, it is customary for the seller to pay the entire brokerage fee.

I personally recommend using a buyer's broker. If you're new to real estate investing, contact a few brokers and use them to learn and to build a network. I also recommend letting your broker know which *specific* types of properties you're looking to purchase, the specific neighborhoods you're targeting, and how much money you want to invest.

All that being said, you shouldn't rely too much on brokers or give them too much information. Don't let a broker negotiate on your behalf. And early on in the negotiation process, don't let the broker know exactly how much you're willing to pay, or what you intend to do with the property. Also, don't merely accept what your broker is telling you about a property. Do your own research, and see if his claims can be verified.

Before making real estate negotiations, find out what the seller's motivation is for selling, and really know what he wants out of the deal. Great negotiators get what they want by helping the other party get what they want.

Also, don't be concerned with how much a seller paid for the property. Be concerned with how much you should pay for it.

This brings up another important matter: Don't let your ego get in the way of a deal. Focus on making advantageous deals, not on personal issues and efforts to gain a vain victory over brokers and owners.

Patience is also important. Granted, there are certain situations where you might need to act quickly. But in general, don't rush while you negotiate, and don't make a follow up offer before you receive a response on your current offer.

Also, it's usually best not to offer to split the difference between your asking price and the seller's price. Instead, wait for the seller to make that proposition.

The P & S Agreement, Escrow, Contingency, and Due Diligence

After settling on a price with a seller, the two of you sign a contract for a purchase-and-sale (P&S) agreement and then open escrow. (Keep in mind that in large deals, a non-legal document called the letter of interest or letter of commitment is signed before the P&S is prepared.) The P&S includes information like the sale price, amount of deposits, due diligence period, contingencies, and date of the closing of escrow. The two parties usually settle on an escrow period in the neighborhood of 60 days—and at the end of that period, the buyer delivers the purchase price minus any deposits and escrow, and he receives the recorded deed of trust. The seller takes the property off the market, and then the buyer goes through the due diligence process.

According to the P&S Agreement, the contract is not complete until contingency is satisfied—meaning that if the buyer's expectations are not met during a specified contingency period, he can back out of the deal and get his deposit back.

The most common types of contingencies are inspection contingencies and loan approval contingencies.

An *inspection contingency* lets the buyer inspect the property and its documents provided by the owner, as well as check city records regarding the property. If the buyer finds defects, he can either (a) walk away from the deal and have his deposit returned, (b) request that the seller remedy the problem, or (c) buy the property "as is" at a reduced price negotiated between the two parties.

A *loan approval contingency* gives the buyer 60 to 90 days to apply for a loan. If he doesn't get a loan in that time, he must show the seller that he made a reasonable effort to obtain one.

In the due diligence process, the buyer physically examines the property in a thorough manner, with experts if needed, checking for any problems with plumbing, electrical systems, heating, air conditioning, the roof, and the building's structure. He also checks to see if the property has environmental hazards related to lead paint, asbestos, mold, underground heating oil and radon, etc. (Keep in mind that these types of hazards are way more common in older buildings. For instance, asbestos was in common use at one time, but was discontinued entirely in the late 70s.)

During the due diligence process, the buyer may talk to the tenants (with pre-approval of the seller), insurers, contractors, engineers, attorneys, and banks. He can also request that the broker provide him with any available documents related to the building—for instance, leases, the last three years' worth of operating statements, the last two years' worth of water, gas, and electricity bills, certificates of occupancy, surveys, building drawings, environmental reports, insurance agreements, and contracts for services like trash removal, cable T.V., elevator, and pest control. The owner may not have some of these documents, but it is better to ask. In all commercial leases except apartment buildings, the owner must provide you with documents known as estoppel certificates—one for each tenant. An estoppel certificate verifies that a tenant's current rental rate and terms are in fact what the owner is claiming they are. It also states if any tenants have rent due.

I recommend obtaining as much information as possible. Make sure you check the leases, certificate of occupancy, square footage, title exceptions, and zoning. Also go to the local city hall and study all the available data about the property—including a file of any violations the property might have.

Some people like to consult an attorney during the due diligence process. However, if you want to keep attorney fees to a minimum, you can perform the due diligence on your own, and then consult with an attorney before removing the contingencies.

Upon the completion of the due diligence process, you can determine whether you want to go through with purchasing the building as is, or if you want to exercise your contractual rights to (a) back out of the deal and get your deposit back, (b) request that the seller make modifications to the building, or (c) request that the owner give you a discount on the purchase price. The last two options are renegotiations that should be handled through your broker.

Title

A title is a document that shows evidence of ownership. When purchasing a property, you should use a title company that will search public records and determine whether the property's title is "clean," or if that title is "clouded" due to adverse claims on it through liens, easements, encroachment, or zoning.

A **lien** basically states that a property owes money to a creditor. Liens are filed by creditors, and recorded in county registrars.

There are two types of liens against a property. *Consensual liens* involve a deed of trust or mortgage. Non-Consensual liens include tax liens by the government for unpaid taxes, mechanic's liens by parties who have done work on the building and not been paid in full, and judgement liens imposed to secure for payment of a judgment.

The outstanding liens must be removed by the seller from the title before a deal is closed and the property is transferred to the buyer.

An **easement** is a right that someone has to access, pass, or use a property. Most easements are known as "utility easements," and allow passage through a property for utility services such as water, electric (either aerial or underground), gas, telephone and cable, sewage and storm drainage.

If you are buying a vacant lot for development, watch out for all the utility easements, because you may not be able to build over an easement area. All the easements are shown on property title.

An **encroachment** involves something protruding from an adjacent property into your property. An encroachment may be visible at the property line or may be underground.

A surveyor will show both easement and encroachment if he surveys the property.

Title problems do not usually kill a deal. If the title has issues, use an experienced real estate attorney to handle any corrections that need to be made by the seller.

A title company can also sell you a title policy that insures the title is free from certain types of defects or encumbrances. Your Purchase and Sale agreement will state the title guarantees and exceptions that are part of the transaction.

In general, all the liens, easements and encroachments, if any, are reflected in the title. Some "clouds" may appear in the title that are mostly errors, misfiled, or lien release that was not recorded. All that must be cleared by the title company and insured with the exceptions that are approved by the buyer.

Financing

Leverage

If you want to maximize the returns you earn as a real estate investor, you need to make low down payments, and borrow most of the purchase price from a bank or other source.

Let's say you buy a property for $90,000 of your own money, and you spend another $10,000 on repairs and renovations—making your initial investment $100,000. You own the building for five years—and over that time, the building has an operating profit of $40,000. Then you sell the property for $140,000. That means you made $40,000 in operating profits, and another $40,000 on the sale of the property (before broker fees). That's $80,000 in profits off of an initial investment of $100,000—which is an 80% return on your money over 5 years, or 16% per year.

Now, suppose instead of buying that building entirely with your own money, you only put $50,000 in the deal, and you borrow the other $50,000 from the bank at a 5% interest rate. In five years, you pay $12,500 in interest. (You'll also make some payments on the principal—but that doesn't affect your actual operating profit). In five years, you make $40,000 in operating profits, minus $12,500 in interest payments—which leaves $27,500. You then sell the property for $140,000. In other words, you made $27,500 in operating profit, and $40,000 off the sale of the property. That's a $67,500 profit total off of an initial investment of $50,000—which works out to a 135% return on your money over 5 years, or 27% per year.

The more you borrow, the higher your return becomes. After all—you borrow money at a 5% interest rate, but you use that money to earn a return of well over 5%.

Of course, borrowing money adds the risk of running into financial difficulties if your cash flow becomes negative due to a weak economy, reduced rents, increased vacancy rates, and/or increased expenses. If you do not have cash reserves and you miss your mortgage payments, your property might go into foreclosure.

But in many cases, it's best to go ahead and borrow money. Analyze your overall financial situation and goals, and determine what type of financing is right for you. If you want to take a more conservative approach to borrowing, here's what I recommend. Run a few calculations, and figure out if you will have the ability to keep your property afloat should its rental revenue decrease by 30%. In other words, if your building is cash flow negative for a while, will you be able to draw funds from other sources and continue paying the mortgage, property taxes, and other expenses until the economy picks up again?

Your Credit Score

Since borrowing power is so significant in real estate, it's important to make sure that you maintain a high credit score. When you have good credit, lenders will not only approve you for loans, they'll also give you more money relative to your down payment, lower interest rates, and more favorable loan terms in general.

Keep in mind that different lenders have different loan plans and policies, and even if you do have a high credit score, you cannot dictate certain terms to a bank if they do not offer them. In such a case, you must go to another lender.

Credit scores are based on an individual's credit profile, borrowing habits, and payback habits. The majority of people have a credit score of 600 to 800—and it can be hard to get a quality loan if your score isn't at least 700.

You can check your credit score for free at certain websites or from certain mortgage companies.

If your score is low, you can take some measures to increase it. If you have a dispute over a minor bill, it is generally best to just go ahead and pay the bill, as opposed to having that bill reported, and getting in the way of you getting a real estate loan.

Keep in mind that even if you pay all your bills on time, your credit score might be somewhat low if you have many maxed out credit cards.

If you have a low credit score, you still might be able to get a loan by explaining the circumstances to a lender, and providing documentation and the like in order to demonstrate that the score is misleading.

If you want to get loans at favorable terms, it also helps to show lenders that you have some sort of steady income, you've lived at the same place for a long period of time, and you have experience managing real estate investments

If no one is willing to give you a loan, you can still explore other options like having your spouse use his/her good credit to get a loan, bringing in another person to cosign the loan, working with a partner who has good credit, or finding a real estate deal in which the owner carries the loan--.i.e. an OWC / Owner Will Carry deal.

Types of Loans

There are a variety of loan structures available in the market, but no matter what type you finance with, the interest rate is a key figure. Lenders base their interest rates on nationally published rates like the prime, 11 District, 12 MAT, Libor, and US Treasury Note.

Many loans have a fixed interest rate, which means your monthly mortgage payment will stay the same throughout the life of the loan. Some loans have an adjustable rate that changes periodically according to an interest rate index specified in the contract. There's no simple rule for determining whether you should go for a fixed rate or adjustable rate loan. However, if you want a more conservative investment with a more predictable cash flow, then a fixed rate loan obviously offers that advantage. If, on the other hand, you want to speculate on interest rates and you think they're going to go down, then an adjustable rate loan is preferable.

Getting a Loan

If you're trying to obtain a loan by yourself, it helps to have a good relationship with the bank loan officer. If you don't, you might want to bring in a loan broker to handle some of the work.

Financing a real estate purchase involves dealing with the bank in two stages. Early on in this process, during your preliminary studies of the property, you discuss the potential purchase with a loan officer or broker, and determine what type of financing is available. Stage two comes after you sign the P&S agreement. At this time, you get a bank commitment or letter of interest that requires you to pay the necessary starting fees for the bank to process the loan. The bank will appraise the property, check the title, perform an environmental study, and check the net operating income—and they will do all of these things at your expense.

When you go to a bank to borrow money, you have to sign two sets of papers: a promissory note and a deed of trust (or mortgage).

The note specifies the amount owed, the monthly payments, the loan's due date, and all of the other conditions of the loan. The deed of trust is a security agreement that gives the lender the right to foreclose on the property in the event of a loan default.

When dealing with a bank, personal liability is an important issue. If the economy weakens and your property's expenses exceed its revenues, you have to either infuse cash every month to make up for the shortage, or default on your mortgage and face foreclosure. If you have personally guaranteed your loan, the lender has the legal right to not only take the property, but also go after your personal assets. If, however, you have a "non-recourse" loan, then your personal assets are protected, and the bank only has the rights to the property.

Some lenders offer loans that are assumable. This means you can sell the property and have the new owner take over the loan. It's to your advantage to have an assumable loan, since it can make your property more desirable to potential buyers.

In some cases, you might be able to obtain financing from the property's seller instead of from a bank. Seller financing generally is provided with a shorter term than of other lenders, but also offers many advantages—for instance, a lower down payment, lower credit standards, less paperwork, and a quicker sale.

Mortgage Payments

A mortgage payment is applied to both principal and interest. Every month, the same amount is due—but early in the loan, more of your payment is applied to the interest, and towards the end of the loan, more of your payment is applied to the principal. At the end of the year, your lender will report how much principal and interest you have paid—two figures that will affect your net income for tax purposes, and determine how much you owe in income taxes.

Home loans are usually amortized for 30 years, and due in 30 years. Commercial loans are amortized for 20 or 25 years, but due before that. Let me put it this way. With a home loan, there is no balance due at the end of the 30 year term. All the principal has already been paid over the 30 years. With commercial loans, the loan might be amortized for 25 years, but due in 10 (i.e. a "25/10" loan). That means you make payments based on the loan running for 25 years—but after you make 10 years' worth of payments, the loan is due, and you're obligated to pay the balance on the principal.

Refinancing

A borrower has the option to pay off a loan before the due date. He might elect to do this because he wants to sell the property, he wants to refinance the loan, or he wants to take out a bigger loan on the property.

In most cases, if you pay off a loan early, you will be charged a prepayment penalty specified in the loan agreement. This penalty varies greatly from loan to loan.

Refinancing a loan is a fairly common practice. You might, for instance, take out a loan when interest rates are high—and then a few years later, they might drop considerably. You can replace your existing 8% interest rate loan with one that charges 5% (, if it makes sense to do so based on the prepayment penalty you will incur).

You can also refinance simply to raise some additional cash. Suppose you purchase a property for $900,000, $600,000 of which you borrow from a bank. Over the next several years, the property's value increases to $1.5 million, and you want to increase the size of your loan on the property. You borrow $1 million from another bank, you pay off the original $600,000 loan, and you use the remaining $400,000 to purchase another property and/or to enhance the first property. This process of taking out a larger loan on your existing property and getting cash in hand is referred to as a "cash out." Keep in mind that there are no income taxes due when you make a cash out.

Forms of Ownership

There are several forms of real estate ownership. When deciding which one is right for you, you should consider the nature of the investment, how long you intend to own the property, what is required from you and any partners you might have, and various legal and tax ramifications.

Individual or Joint ownership

Individual ownership is the ordinary way of owning a property, the same way you would own a car or a TV. Joint ownership is like individual ownership, only there are multiple owners of the property. Joint ownership is usually used when a couple buys a house or condominium.

Joint Venture

A joint venture involves two or more entities having a predetermined investing and profit sharing arrangement. Many large real estate projects are structured under a joint venture which will cease to exist at the end of the project.

A partnership is a type of joint venture with more government ruling and reporting. In a **general partnership**, each individual is responsible for all of the partnership's liabilities and debts. In a **limited partnership**, there's one or more general partners who run the business and take on the debts and liabilities, and there's one or more limited partners who have no authority in the venture, and are not personally liable for anything. The most money a limited partner can lose is the money he invested into the project.

Partnerships report their income to the federal government, and then the individual partners pay their taxes separately.

Corporation

A corporation is an independent entity, and its ownership is split up among individuals known as shareholders. Shareholders have no personal liability, and they also have no authority aside from the fact that they can elect the corporation's board of directors. A **C corporation** is a regular corporation that pays corporate taxes on its profits. On top of that, each shareholder must also pay his own personal income tax on any dividends (profit payouts) he receives from corporation. A **subchapter S corporation** is like a C corporation, only its corporate profits are nontaxable, and directly transferred to the shareholder, who must then pay personal income taxes.

LLC (Limited Liability Company)

An LLC offers the legal protection of a corporation and the tax benefits of a partnership. An LLC does not pay income taxes on the company level—and its "members" (as in, partners or shareholders) are, for the most part, not personally responsible for liabilities and debts of the LLC.

Management

Real estate investors can either manage their investment, or outsource the managerial duties to a real estate management company.

No matter which option you choose, you should understand what is involved in real estate management.

In order to manage a property, you must collect rents and other payments due, pay bills (mortgage, utilities, insurance, real estate taxes, services performed, employees, repairs, supplies, etc.), maintain the property and ensure that it remains in good condition, enforce all the rules and regulations under the tenant lease, comply with all codes and regulations, lease vacant units directly or via brokers, and prepare the monthly financial statements.

Management companies charge about 5% of the rent collected, and they also charge additional fees for leasing and for major repairs.

There are many advantages to using a management company—most notably, your job is way less demanding and time consuming, and you benefit from their knowledge and experience. Also, large national management companies are great for retail properties, since they tend to be the best at getting very desirable anchor tenants (as in Starbucks, Whole Foods Market, The Apple Store, etc.)

If you decide to hire a management company to run your building, you should interview the person in the company who will do the actual work in your building. If he seems to be the right fit for the job, sign a management contract that you are able to cancel with a 30-day notice. Don't make any long term commitments.

Keep in mind that even with having a management company on board, you still have to supervise the work, as well as make various decisions regarding cash flow, vacancies, capital improvements, refinancing, insurance carriers, new leases, and taxes. Also, in some management agreements there is a certain clause that any expense costing over a certain dollar amount has to be authorized by the owner.

If you manage the property on your own, you'll not only save money on management fees, you'll also have the opportunity to learn a great deal about real estate. Furthermore, even good management companies might not know that much about your building specifically, and they might be too busy with other projects to give your property the proper attention.

Regardless of who manages your property, you should take a proactive role when it comes to selecting tenants and determining the terms of their lease.

Tenants

A real estate owner's job is not to merely find tenants and sign leases and renewals with them in order to keep vacancies to a minimum. Your property will be significantly affected by the quality of the tenants. High quality tenants are a valuable asset, and you should take measures to attract and retain them.

Having a good screening process is an integral part of this. Rental applicants must be screened properly, in order to determine the likelihood that they'll pay rent consistently, behave well, and not damage the property.

Start by obtaining the applicant's credit report through a credit company, studying his credit history as well as his application form, and calling the individuals listed as references. If the applicant looks good on paper, then interview him thoroughly in person.

During this first meeting with a prospective tenant, go out of your way to establish a good relationship with him.

Be cordial. Do not try to establish yourself as a figure of authority.

When people deal with landlords, they tend to feel uneasy and suspicious, due to their perception of a landlord as a big guy who makes a living by taking advantage of the little guy. If a person has that attitude towards you, he might turn into the type of tenant who starts making all sorts of unreasonable complaints and demands—and when you point out that you are not contractually required to meet his demands, he will probably feel like you are basically lying. In other words, if you do not gain the trust of a tenant early on in the leasing process, your relationship with him might become hostile and adversarial, and of course, high maintenance on your part.

If you try to let the tenant know that you're the boss on day one, he might not react well. A tenant is not your employee; in fact, he's more like your customer. For the most part, you should treat him accordingly.

I even recommend doing something extra for the tenant at the beginning and sometimes during the term of the lease, even though you are not contractually obligated to do so. Be sure to remind the tenant that you did not have to do it according to the contract.

As a real estate owner, aside from having high quality tenants, another aim of yours should be to appropriately deal with all tenant complaints. In most cases, this involves dealing with complaints in a prompt manner. Do not be a landlord who frequently takes too long to deal with such matters.

If you have a tenant who is highly irrational and makes complaints that are out of the ordinary, start exploring ways to have that tenant removed.

Types of Real Estate and Leases

Leases can be signed for as little as one month (with month-to-month options of renewals) all the way to ten years or longer.

Leases specify how much the rent will be increased over the duration of the lease—for instance, a 4 year lease might state that the rent will go up 3% per year, or that the rate of increase will be decided by the Consumer Price Index, which measures changes in inflation and the cost of living.

At the expiration of the term of the lease, the lease automatically converts to a month-to-month deal, optional for both the owner and the occupant, unless a new lease is negotiated and signed for a new term.

Again, keep in mind that many apartment buildings are subject to rent control laws, which give the tenant an option of renewing the lease with a fairly modest increase in rent.

There are six main types of real estate: apartment buildings, offices, retail properties, industrial properties, hotels, and single family homes. They differ greatly in terms of pricing, operation, tenancy, and marketing.

Apartment buildings

Apartment buildings tend to be a good fit for most investors, because relative to the other types of real estate, they provide a stable and predictable cash flow, they're less dependent on the state of the economy, and their values seldom drop that much. On the other hand, running an apartment can be somewhat demanding, as it involves dealing with numerous tenants, as well as health codes, fire and safety codes, making a variety of repairs, and ensuring that heat and water are available to the units, and all units are in a condition that would be deemed "habitable" according to local laws. Furthermore, some apartments are subject to rent control laws, which can make it very difficult to raise rents to their market value. Also, although apartment buildings tend to perform well in cities that attract new residents, they don't do so well in regions with slowly growing or declining populations, where they often have a tough time competing with low priced single family homes.

Apartment leases tend to be short term--as in two years, one year, or even month-to-month. The leases often require the tenant to pay his own utility expenses. However, if there is a utility in the building that has a common/shared meter, the property owner pays for that utility (, and passes the cost onto the tenant in the form of a slightly higher rental rate).

Retail Properties

Retail properties are usually easier to manage than apartment buildings, and their performance is tied to the business performance of the tenants. In many cases, a retail property will have difficulty maximizing profits unless it has at least one big name tenant—in other words, a tenant that's part of a major, established, successful retail chain. These tenants, known in the real estate industry as "anchor tenants," tend to drive traffic to the other businesses, and greatly increase the value of the entire property.

Managing a retail property involves dealing with an environment that changes due to not only the economy, but also trends and technology—for example, in the 90s and early 2000s, retail properties focused on attracting and meeting the needs of video rental stores, bookstores, and medium sized supermarkets; whereas nowadays, the retail environment has ventured away from those types of businesses.

Retail leases are usually for five to ten years, and involve a tenant paying a base rent, plus a pro rata share (the tenant's square footage divided by the building's usable square footage) for operating costs, real estate taxes, and utilities. This is referred to as a Triple Net (NNN) Lease. Some retail leases use a percentage rent, which has the tenant pay a base rent, plus a percentage of his sales that go over a certain predetermined figure.

Big name tenants often seek longer leases, since they invest more money in setting up the business. It's usually advantageous for an owner to be flexible with such tenants, and allow them to dictate certain lease terms—as in, duration of the lease, square footage, and even to some extent, rent per square foot.

With smaller businesses, it's generally better to sign shorter leases (5 years max), should you want to (a) increase rents later because of a strengthened economy, (b) renovate the building, or (c) combine two units.

Office Buildings

Investing in office buildings is a bit trickier than investing in other types of real estate. Offices are more sensitive to economic changes—and in down markets, their cash flow can decrease so much, that the owner will have difficulty making loan payments. Furthermore, in most regions in the US, the current supply of office space exceeds the demand. (Technological advances and the outsourcing of jobs to other countries have made the US economy shift away from office spaces to a major extent.)

Office spaces usually have a lease term of two to five years, and use a gross lease which has the landlord pay for operating costs, real estate taxes, and in most cases, utilities. The landlord also usually covers expenses that the tenant incurs when the tenant improves his space in various ways.

Other

Industrial properties cater to tenants who produce, warehouse, or distribute goods, and require dock areas for loading and unloading.

Industrial leases often run for two to five years, and may either be in the form of a NNN lease or a gross lease.

Hotels are vastly different from other types of properties, as they are service oriented, and also require way more in the way of day-to-day management.

Single Family Homes are vastly different from other types of real estate. For starters, a home's valuation has quite a bit to do with financially intangible factors like aesthetic appeal. The income produced by the property is deemphasized. Furthermore, single family homes are subject to unique income tax laws that give the owner a tax break should he also reside in the property. In a certain sense, single family homes hardly even fall under the category of commercial real estate.

CAP Rate and Return on Investment

If you want to properly analyze the listing price of a property, two important figures to look at are **CAP rate** and **Return on Investment**.

Suppose an apartment building is listed for $1 million. It's expected to generate $100,000 a year in rental revenues and incur $30,000 in operating expenses, leaving $70,000 in net operating income. To calculate the CAP rate, you take the net operating income, and divide it by the price. In this case, it's $70,000 divided by $1 million, which works out to 0.07/7%, or "7 CAP."

Now we'll calculate the Return on Investment, which is like CAP rate, only it factors in a loan. Instead of paying $1 million of your own money, you pay $250,000 down, and borrow the remaining $750,000. And your mortgage payment is $50,000 a year (on a 5.5% loan over 30 years). The property generates $100,000 a year from rent received, and has $30,000 in expenses. It also has $50,000 in annual mortgage payments. That leaves $20,000 in cash flow. The NOI / Net Operating Income is calculated by taking the cash flow, and dividing it by the down payment. In this case, that's $20,000 in cash flow divided by a $250,000 down payment—which works out to 0.08, or an 8% return on investment.

In other words, CAP is your expected annual return if you buy the property with your own money, and ROI is the amount of cash in hand your investment will yield annually if you borrow money to purchase the property.

Now, suppose you own a building and you're not sure how much it's worth. You do some research and find out that similar properties are selling at 9 CAP. Your property has a Net Operating Income of $100,000. If you apply that same CAP to your building, you can calculate the approximate value by taking the $100,000 in Net Operating Income, and dividing it by 0.09—which works out to $1,111,111.11

Real Estate CAP rates tend to range anywhere from 2 to 18. If a property is in great condition and it's in a desirable location with a strong regional economy where growth is projected, then the property will have a very low CAP rate. Properties with high CAP rates tend to be in poor condition and located in areas that are deteriorated and deteriorat*ing*.

Development

Real estate investing involves either buying an existing property, or buying a piece of vacant land to develop. I have covered the former topic throughout this book, and I will briefly cover development in this chapter.

Developing land is a far more intricate process than buying an existing property, due to factors such as:

- *Time and timing.* There is generally a span of about three years between the time you search for land to buy and the time you complete the development process. Many changes can occur over this time and upset your calculations.

- *The Market.* You are creating a new product in the market, and must make assumptions about the income and the value of the finished product a few years from now.

- *Variety of tasks and people.* You will need to deal with a very wide variety of people, such as architects, engineers, city clerks, and contractors.

- *Personal liability.* In order to secure a loan for land development, you will need to make a personal guarantee on the loan, and expose your personal assets to your potential business losses.

- *Time and budget constraints.* Land development involves deadlines and budgets to meet, and if you fail to meet them, you will be exposed to major financial losses.

If you are a beginner in real estate investing, I strongly recommended you avoid land development. Land development requires extensive real estate experience. First purchase existing properties, and after you have familiarized yourself with the business, you will be better equipped to deal with all the new variables involved with developing new properties.

Attorneys and Legal Issues

I highly recommend that all real estate investors use the services of a qualified real estate attorney (not a general purpose attorney) when making a real estate transaction. It's generally not necessary to go with the best or most expensive attorney in town; rather, just find one who can handle the work related to your specific objectives.

Confine the use of attorneys primarily to the legal aspects of a deal. The attorney's main job is to examine all the contract, the title, the escrow instructions, and various other documents and issues related to the property and the other party, and to report his findings to you in a thorough and timely manner. It's generally not a good idea to involve him in appraising a property and negotiating for it on your behalf, or to have him make business decisions.

One thing to note is that the business advice of an attorney tends to be very conservative. Attorneys more or less see it as part of their job to take conservative stances. An attorney can provide some information regarding what the risks are—but ultimately, you have to decide what risks are suitable for you as a real estate investor.

Over the course of my own career, I have sometimes gone with a conservative approach, but other times, I have opted to go with options that were not conservative at all, and not in line with an attorney's business recommendations. My decisions were based on what I felt was suitable for me at the time and given the specific situation. Making these types of assessments requires a certain degree of sophistication and complexity in your style of thinking and analyzing. Again—a real estate attorney typically does not really provide much that is conducive to this, and merely favors the conservative approach. A real estate investor must take things to the next level and get a sense of what really suits his investing goals.

Income Taxes

Real estate profits are generally subject to income taxes—however, there are various income tax laws that allow real estate owners to defer or even avoid some of these taxes.

(In all cases, whether you're deferring taxes or avoiding them, spend some time researching tax laws to verify that the options mentioned are available to you.)

If you're selling a property at a profit and you want to use the proceeds to purchase a new property, you can make a *1031 Exchange* (named after Section 1031 of the IRS code) and defer taxes on the gain. For instance, if you buy a property for $100,000 and sell it for $150,000, you take the $150,000 and apply it to the purchase of a new property, and you don't pay income taxes on the $50,000 profit you made on the original property. You only pay taxes when you "cash out"—i.e. you sell your existing property without making another 1031 exchange and buying another property. Keep in mind that in order to make a 1031 exchange, you are required to purchase the second property within a certain number of days after selling the first one. Furthermore, the new property's purchase price must be equal to or greater than the price of the property being sold—otherwise, you are subject to taxes due on the difference in prices.

Aside from making 1031 exchanges, another way to defer income taxes is to factor in *depreciation* when you calculate your property's annual income. You deduct the estimated decrease in the value of the property (not including the land) due to wear, tear, and obsolescence. The depreciation period for a commercial property is 29 years, and that of a single family residence is 31.5 years. For example, if you buy a commercial property for $1 million of which $800,000 is assessed for the building and the remaining $200,000 is assessed for the land, you may depreciate the property annually in the amount of $800,000 divided by 29, or $27,580 (per year for 29 years). So, if your property generates $50,000 in annual income (before depreciation) and you calculate $27,580 worth of annual depreciation, you deduct the depreciation from the income, and you only pay taxes on the $22,420 in net income. Now, suppose you do this for five years. You deduct $27,580 a year in depreciation, or $137,900 total. For tax purposes, you said, "I bought this property for $1 million, and now it's worth $137,900 less than that. It's worth $862,100." If you then go ahead and sell the property for more than $862,100, it counts as a profit. If you sell the property for your original purchase price of $1 million, you show a profit of $137,900. In such a case, over the course of five years, you show a loss on paper of $137,900, and then a gain on paper of $137,900. This is all just a way to defer paying taxes—paying taxes later instead of earlier.

Deferring taxes is financially advantageous for an investor, because it's like getting an interest free loan on money that you use to earn a return.

There are also some ways to avoid taxes altogether. For instance, people who own and sell their place of residence are exempt from taxes on gains under $500,000 for couples or $250,000 for a single person, as long as they live in that home for a minimum of two years. You can take advantage of this law by continuously purchasing fixer upper homes, living in them while you improve their condition, and selling them for gains of up to $500,000/$250,000 without paying any taxes.

Home ownership in general is often a good option for real estate investors. Advantages to owning your own residence include:

- A deduction of interest payments on your personal income tax return

- A deduction of real estate taxes (unlike commercial real estate).

- A low required down payment (relative to the down payments for commercial real estate loans)

- If you're new to real estate, purchasing a home and making mortgage payments can provide you with valuable experience on the workings of the real estate industry.

All that being said, your residence is not an income producing property, and that being the case, your financial approach to buying and owning your home should be more conservative than your approach with other types of real estate. I would say that no more than 25% of your gross income should go toward your home mortgage, property taxes, and insurance. Also, I would not recommend having a great deal of debt on your home.

When to Sell

Most people have heard advice like "buy low and sell high," or perhaps, "buy when the market is bad, and sell when the market is good." But in truth, it is difficult and often impossible to determine when the economy is peaking or bottoming. Some people sell high after the market shoots up 30% in one year—and yet, a surge like that might be followed by a similar or even greater one the following year. Likewise, some people buy low after a steady, long term decline in values—and yet, the market might remain weak and get weaker for years after that.

When it comes to selling a property, I believe that the main reasons to sell are:

- You have encountered certain types of problems, such as disputes with your partners

- The numbers (return on equity, etc.) do not justify owning the property anymore

- You have exhausted all of the property's major opportunities / potential

- You need the money for other reasons

In trying to determine whether you should sell, consider the disadvantages of selling:

- Broker fees

- Legal fees

- Closing costs

- Prepayment penalties built in your loan, if any

- Potential difficulty in finding another place to invest your money

- Taxes due (including capital gains taxes and/or deferred taxes)

- Surrendering any accumulated state tax benefits associated with holding real estate over time (For example, in California, an owner's annual property tax due increases only 2% per year beginning from the year he purchased the property—so if you own a property that appreciates faster than 2% per year, you benefit. You lose this benefit when you sell the property.)

- The time and effort required to sell a property

Perform a broad examination before deciding to sell. I know many people who sold a property mainly because of the excitement generated from its value appreciation and/or a broker's encouragement, without properly assessing the total advantages and disadvantages of selling.

Also realize that you can refinance a property that has appreciated in value, and thereby generate additional funds for other real estate investments.

Putting it All Together

In this chapter, I am going to bring up a wide variety of real estate concepts and terms as I analyze a hypothetical real estate scenario. This should give you a better sense of how some of what I've covered so far in this book applies to typical real estate deals.

Mr. Simpson owns a property, and puts it on the market with a listing price of $100,000. Mr. Bailey is interested in purchasing the property.

The data sheet provided by Simpson, the seller, indicates that the property collects $10,000 in rental revenue per year, and has expenses of $3,500 per year.

Bailey, the potential buyer, provides the preliminary data to a bank, and the loan officer offers a $70,000 loan with the following terms: a 4% fixed interest rate, and a 25/7 structure—as in, the loan is amortized over 25 years, but the total is due after 7 years via a payment known as a "balloon payment."

The major financial numbers pertaining to this property are as follows:

Income 10,000.00
Operating Expense (3,500.00)
Net Operating Income 6,500.00
Mortgage Payments (4433.83)
Cash Flow 2066.17

CAP Rate = 6,500/100,000 = 0.065 or 6.5
Return on Investment = 2066.17/30,000 = .0689 or 6.89%

Bailey compares these figures with those of similar properties for sale or similar properties sold in the last few months. He also performs a preliminary inspection of the property, taking note, among other things, of the building's condition, its potential, and the quality of the neighborhood.

He decides to buy the property. Simpson chooses an escrow company, and Bailey is fine with the choice. Bailey deposits 3% of the purchase price, or $3,000, into escrow. Bailey and Simpson agree on the following terms: a 60-day closing, a 15 day contingency for inspection, and a 30 day contingency for the loan. All of these terms are included in the escrow instructions which are signed by both parties.

During the first 15 days after entering escrow, Bailey reviews a preliminary title report given to him by the escrow company, and he also performs a physical inspection of the property.

(If he is not satisfied with the property's condition or the details included in the title and the other paperwork, he can notify Simpson that he is not interested in making the transaction, after which Bailey gets his $3000 deposit back and the deal is dropped from escrow.)

During the first 30 days after entering escrow, Bailey seeks financing for the deal. On the bank's loan application form, he states that he wants the property to be vested in his own name—in other words, he wants to buy the property as an individual, as opposed to doing so under a set up entity. Bailey has a credit score of 750. Bailey is approved by the bank via a letter of interest that specifies all major loan conditions, including the loan amount of $70,000 (as in, 70% of the property's value), the fixed interest rate of 4%, and the loan due date of 7 years. The terms are all contingent upon the bank ordering an appraisal and performing other studies such as environmental reports (if needed) at Bailey's expense.

Bailey agrees to the terms of the letter of interest. The bank appraises the building at $100,000, and determines that the building has no major issues environmental or otherwise.

(If the bank had appraised the property for less than $100,000, [and consequently changed the loan terms], or if they had found hazardous material or structural problems [and refused to loan the money unless the problem was corrected], Bailey would've had the option of (a) dropping the escrow and getting back his $3,000 deposit [provided that he would send the bank's letter to Simpson through the escrow company], or (b) seeking to go through with the deal, but under new conditions negotiated with Simpson. [Keep in mind that in most cases, it's very difficult for a buyer and seller to resolve issues related to environmental matters while a deal is in escrow.])

Bailey is ready to go through with the deal. The results of his physical inspection were satisfactory, he is fine with the title report and other documents, and $70,000 in financing has been obtained. The bank notifies the escrow company that it is ready to send funds in the amount of $70,000. The escrow company notifies Simpson and Bailey that the deal is to be completed. They tell Bailey he needs to (a) deposit the remaining amount of $27,000 (keep in mind that this figure factors in Bailey's initial $3,000 deposit), and (b) show up in escrow to sign the note and the trust deed* prepared by the bank which reflects all items in the bank's letter of interest. As for Simpson, he needs to sign the grant deed.

(*In some states, different documents are involved in this process. For instance, a mortgage is used instead of a trust deed.)

After Simpson and Bailey perform those tasks, the funds are placed in escrow and the deal is closed. The bank immediately places a lien on the property in the amount of $70,000 and records it with the recording office of the county where the property is located.

The escrow company receives a fee of $1,000 for processing the deal: Bailey pays $500, and Simpson pays $500. Upon closing the deal, the escrow company pays Simpson the amount of $100,000.

Bailey owns the property. After a few years, the building's value has increased considerably due to increases in local real estate values, as well as improvements and rent increases instituted by Bailey.

Bailey needs to raise $25,000 cash for personal uses. He determines that the building is worth about $140,000. He comes to this conclusion based on sales of comparable buildings. He also calculates the building's value via its operating results. The building is collecting $12,000 in annual rental revenues, and has annual operating expenses of 3,700, yielding an annual Net Operating Income of $7,100. Also, although the property had a CAP rate of 6.5 when it was purchased, changes in the local real estate market and improvements to his property have made the property worth more relative to its income. Bailey feels that a suitable CAP rate for the property is now 6. The estimated value of the property is the Net Operating Income (NOI) of $8,300 divided by the CAP rate of 0.06, which amounts to $138,333.

The property's financial numbers are as follows:

Income 12,000.00
Operating Expense (3,700.00)
Net Operating Income 8,300.00

Mortgage Payment (4433.83)
Cash Flow: 3866.17

Estimated CAP Rate = 6
Appraised Value $138,333

In order for Bailey to raise the $25,000 in funds he seeks, he can either sell the property, refinance the property, or get a second loan.

He doesn't want to sell the property, and refinancing has major drawbacks: it takes two months to refinance, there's a prepayment penalty for paying off the first bank loan before its due date, there are fees associated with the new loan, and interest rates have gone up since the time he purchased the property and got the first loan. That being the case, he decides to keep the original loan and add an additional one. He finds a mortgage company willing to quickly provide him with $25,000 in "hard money." The second loan is interest-only, with no principal payments due. Also, the interest rate on the second loan is 8%, as opposed to 4% for the original loan. This is because (a) interest rates have risen between the time of the first loan and the second loan, and (b) second lenders charge more than first lenders. (The first lender owns the first trust deed [a.k.a. the "senior lien"], while the second lender owns the second trust deed [or the "junior lien"]. The first lender has priority over the second lender in the event that the owner does not make his mortgage payments and is subject to a foreclosure. Since the second lender is more likely to not get paid back in full, the second lender will demand a higher interest rate in the loan terms.)

Bailey gets $25,000 from the second loan. He makes monthly payments on both loans, which reduces the property's cash flow considerably.

Income 12,000.00
Operating Expense (3,700.00)
Net Operating Income 8,300.00
First Mortgage Payment (4433.83)
Second Mortgage Payment (2000.00)
Cash Flow 1866.17

Shortly after Bailey gets the second loan for $25,000, the local real estate market cools off and the national economy also enters a recession. Bailey has to lower rents in the building. He also accumulates a few vacancies. The property's revenues can no longer cover all the loan payments and other building expenses.

Bailey has to make two mortgage payments, cover general building expenses, and also pay property taxes that are due. He opts to not pay his property taxes, since they are lower priority than the other expenses, and he can put off paying them without suffering much in the way of negative consequences.

With non-payment of property taxes, he stays afloat for a while, but the property's rental revenue continues to decrease, and now Bailey cannot make payments on all his loans.

If Bailey stops making payments on the loans, the loans will go into default. At that point, either lender can initiate the foreclosure process—although the first lender has more of a motive to do so. If the first lender does this, it will involve an appraisal of the property, and then a notification to the public and to the second lender that the property will be sold at auction. The property is auctioned via the foreclosure process initiated by the first lender. What happens at that point depends on what the winning bid is. If the winning bid is less than the money owed to the first lender (—by "first lender," technically I mean the owner of the first trust deed), the property is not sold to the winning bidder. Instead, the first lender takes over ownership of the property, and any subsequent lenders are not entitled to any money (either now or later). If the winning bid is more than what is owed to the first lender, the winning bidder takes over the property, the first lender gets whatever they are owed, and any money left over goes to the other lenders, and then to the former owner of the property (in this case, Bailey).

(By the way—lenders have priority based on their order. If for some reason a second trust deed* owner forecloses, the first trust deed owner is still entitled to whatever is owed according to the first loan. If a third trust deed owner forecloses, the first and second trust deed owners are still entitled to whatever they're owed. On the other hand, if the first trust deed owner forecloses, the second and third trust deed owners will only get money if the foreclosure sale amount is sufficient.)

[*Again, keep in mind that some states use a mortgage document instead of a deed of trust.]

Now, getting back to the property in question. It was purchased for $100,000, it increased in value to

$130,000, Bailey took out an additional loan in the amount of $25,000, and then the property value decreased to $65,000.

Let's examine the conditions and positions of everyone and everything involved in this scenario:

The Property is worth $65,000. There are three monetary liens on the property (listed in order of seniority): (1) a property tax lien of about $2,500; (2) a first trust deed of about $67,000 in remaining principal plus $4,000 back interest and legal fees; (3) a second trust deed of $25,000 plus back interest, if any.

Bailey owns a property that has an open market value of $65,000, and has debts amounting to about $100,000. His equity in the property is negative $35,000. The property is cash flow negative—in other words, its revenues cannot cover all of its expenses. He has already stopped making property tax payments, and now he is having trouble making loan payments.

The County Assessor. The county is owed $2,500 in taxes, and that figure is increasing on account of an 18% interest charge on the amount due. Also, the county's lien is ahead of the first and second trust deeds' liens.

However, the county cannot put the property into auction until five years have passed since the first tax default.

The First Lender. The first lender is looking to recoup $67,000 in principle it is owed, along with $4,000 in back interest and legal fees. A foreclosure will yield the first lender an apartment building that is worth $65,000 and owes $2,500 in property taxes. Also, the loan was not personally guaranteed by Bailey, so the first lender cannot go after his personal assets.

The first lender is like most banks in that it is not interested in going through a demanding foreclosure process, nor is it interested in acquiring real estate, especially while the local real estate market is cold. They would prefer to merely negotiate with Bailey and settle for a cash payment of less than what is owed. Another option is for them to merely sell the loan (technically, the thing they sell is referred to as a "note") to another bank or entity that specializes in non-performing loans and foreclosures. In such a case, the loan will be sold at a discount to its face value, the buyer of the loan/note will take over the role of lender, and the terms of the loan and trust deed will remain the same.

The Second Lender. The second lender has $25,000 tied up in the property, but they do not have much of a financial motive to get involved in the matter. If the property were valued at $80,000 instead of $65,000, it's possible the second lender would bid on the property and become the new owner, or maybe purchase the note from the first lender before the initiation of the foreclosure process.

Now, returning to our scenario involving Bailey. He cannot cover the building's expenses by using the building's rental revenue. He determines, however, that it is financially worthwhile to pump some additional money into the investment in order to keep the property afloat. He sells off some other assets he has, and he also reduces his personal expenditures to some extent. This enables him to afford loan payments, and to start paying off the amount due on his $2,500+ property tax bill. Over 32 months, Bailey puts $6,500 into the property. This is an average of just over $200 per month. The economy improves gradually, and by the end of the 32 months, the property becomes cash flow even. A few months later, it is cash flow positive.

A few years later, the property is valued at $160,000. The first loan is now at the end of its seven year term, and the payments made over the seven years have brought the principal due down from $70,000 to $57,000. (The second loan still has $25,000 due, since it is an interest-only loan.)

Bailey initially invested $30,000, and at one point he added $6,500 during a three year recessionary period in order to stave off foreclosure. He owns a $160,000 property with debts of $82,000 ($57,000 on the first loan and $25,000 on the second loan). His equity is $78,000.

Since his loan is due, he refinances it. A bank offers him a loan of 70% of the property's $160,000 value, or $112,000. He uses the money to pay off the $82,000 in principal from the two previous loans. He's left with $30,000 cash (with no income taxes due at the time), along with $48,000 in equity in a $160,000 property.

CONCLUSION

There are ways to make a quick buck in real estate—but in the case of Bailey, real estate was an investment that produced returns over the long run.

A well-rounded real estate investor is always prepared to deal with and ride out the bad days until matters subside.

GLOSSARY

ADJUSTABLE RATE MORTGAGE - A mortgage loan with an interest rate that varies throughout the life of the loan. Typically, the rate is changed periodically (in most cases, annually or monthly) according to an index mentioned in the loan contract.

AMORTIZATION PERIOD - The length of time over which the principal of a mortgage loan is scheduled to be paid down

APPRAISAL - An estimate (made by a qualified professional) of a property's open market value

ASSESSMENT - Taxes and fees charged by the county or municipality against a property

BALLOON PAYMENT - A scheduled payment on the entire principal balance of a mortgage loan. The contract of a loan specifies if and when a balloon payment is due—for instance, a loan contract might include a term stating that a balloon payment is due 7 years after the loan is made.

BUILDING CODES - Regulations to a building structure enforced by local and state laws

BUILDING PERMIT - A document issued by a government regulatory authority that allows a builder to construct or modify a structure

CAP(ITALIZATION) RATE - A figure indicating how much an investor would make (annually) on his money if he were to purchase a certain property without getting a loan. A CAP rate is calculated by taking a property's expected Net Operating Income (NOI) over the next 12 months, and dividing it by the property's asking price.

CLOSING - a meeting between the buyer, seller and lender (or their agents) in which a property and funds legally change hands

CLOUD ON TITLE - A term indicating that there is a problem with the title, and the problem must be cleared before the deal is closed

COMMON AREAS - Parts of a property that are shared by tenants (--for instance, hallways and lobbies)

CONTINGENCY - A defined condition or action that must be satisfactorily met before a real estate contract can become binding

CREDITOR - A person or entity to whom money is owed

DEED - A signed legal document proving ownership of a property

DEBT SERVICE - The periodic principal and interest payments made on a loan

DEFAULT - Breaking an agreement by failing to fulfill an obligation; normally used in reference to a borrower who does not pay his mortgage before the due date

DISCOUNT RATE - The interest rate charged by the Federal Reserve when making loans to member banks

DUE DILIGENCE - Adequate research and other activities that are expected to be performed by a person given the particular circumstances.

ENVIRONMENTAL REPORT - A report prepared by qualified individuals that determines potential environmental hazards within a property or in the property's region

EQUITY - The open market value of an asset minus any current debts owed on that asset

ESCROW - Money (or other assets) held by a third party on behalf of two other parties that are making a transaction

FIXED-RATE MORTGAGE - A mortgage with an interest rate that remains unchanged for the life of the loan

FORECLOSURE - A legal process by which a lender takes control of a property after the owner has failed to make scheduled payments on the property's mortgage

INDUSTRIAL PROPERTY - Factories, warehouses, and other properties used for industrial purposes

LEVERAGE - The impact of using money other than your own

LIMITED LIABILITY - When a shareholder's potential losses are limited to the value of his shares

LIMITED PARTNERSHIP - A partnership that includes (a) one or more partners who are passive and limit their liability to the shares they one, and (b) one or more partners whose liability is not limited to the shares they own

LOAN-TO-VALUE RATIO (LTV) - The ratio between (a) a loan amount (i.e. a mortgage's principal balance), and (b) the current appraised value of a real estate property that backs a loan. The loan-to-value ratio is used in the financial industry in order to assess risk associated with a loan.

MANAGEMENT FEE - Money paid to a property management company for managing a property. In most management contracts, the management fee is calculated monthly by taking a percentage of the property's effective gross income.

MATURITY - A loan's due date; or, more generally, the date or period when a note, loan, transaction, or financial instrument ends, after which it is either renewed, or it is terminated.

MIXED USE - A property containing two or more different uses that are intended to effectively coexist—for instance, an apartment building with retail shops on the first floor

MORTGAGE - A real estate loan document that gives the lender the right to place a lien on the property

NET OPERATING INCOME (NOI) - A property's revenue (money collected) minus operating expenses. Operating expenses include repairs, basic maintenance expenses, property taxes, insurance, property management fees, legal fees, utilities. Mortgage payments, income taxes, tenant improvements (i.e. construction expenses associated with making a unit suitable for a new tenant), leasing commissions, and capital expenditures (i.e. major repairs and replacements) are not included in the category of "operating expenses."

OPERATING EXPENSE - (see Net Operating Income)

PERCENTAGE LEASE - A type of retail store lease whose rent is calculated by taking a certain "base rent" (say, $10,000 a month) and then adding a percentage of the unit's gross sales "overage" (usually 1% to 6% of the gross sales)

PREPAYMENT PENALTY - The fee a borrower pays when he retires a loan prematurely

PRIME RATE - The lowest rate a bank lends money to customers; the prime rate is given to those with the best credit

PRINCIPAL - The amount of debt remaining on a loan

PROPERTY TAX - Taxes a property owner pays to a government; the amount due is a certain percentage of the property's market value according to the government's appraisal

REFINANCE - Replacing an existing loan or loans with a new loan or loans

RENOVATION - Reconstructing a property in a way that brings it up to a "like new" state

RENT ROLL - a document containing information regarding the tenants leasing a property; the document includes the names of the tenants, the areas being leased, certain terms of the lease, and recent and long term payment history

RENTABLE SQUARE FEET (or "Net Leasable Area") - A measure of the amount of floor space that can be rented to tenants

SELF-AMORTIZING MORTGAGE - A mortgage that will retire itself through regular scheduled payments of principal and interest; as opposed to balloon mortgages and interest-only mortgages, which have a balance due at the end of the loan period

TENANT IMPROVEMENTS (TI) - Expenses associated with improving a unit so it is suitable for a current or prospective tenant

TERM - The length of a mortgage

TITLE - A legal document conferring ownership of a property

TRIPLE-NET LEASE (NNN) - A lease that requires tenants to pay a base rent plus property taxes, insurance, and maintenance.